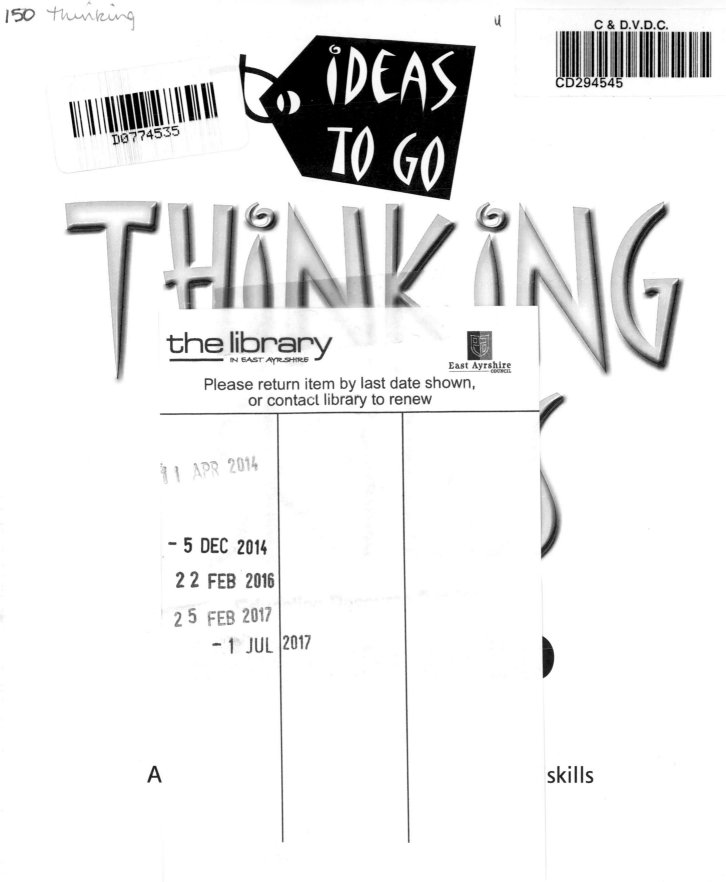

IDEAS
TO GO

THINKING

A   skills

Advisor: Trevor Davies

A & C Black • London

CONTENTS

INTRODUCTION

Today's pupils are the problem solvers of the future. If children are taught factual knowledge only, they tend to respond with conventionally 'correct' answers rather than by exploring creative solutions. All pupils can learn to think critically and creatively. This book provides teachers with straightforward ideas and activities to help pupils develop these skills. The activities make an ideal complement to classroom work across the curriculum. They can be used in isolation, in sequence, or dipped into, as teachers require.

ABOUT THIS BOOK

TEACHERS' FILE

The teachers' file offers advice on how to make make the most of this book. It explains the different types of thinking strategies and how children can benefit from using them. There are ideas for classroom organisation as well as ICT tips, assessment ideas and suggestions for parental involvement.

QUICK STARTS

This section offers activity and game ideas that help to promote children's thinking skills. These activities require little or no preparation and can be used across various learning areas to complement existing lesson plans.

ACTIVITY BANK

Photocopiable activities

The activity bank contains 29 photocopiable activities that cover thinking skills related to fluency, flexibility, imaginative visualisation, originality and elaboration, creative thinking, questioning, and categorising. The activities can be used in any order and can be used by children working individually or in groups.

CHALLENGES

These photocopiable task cards offer creative investigational challenges. They can be given to individual pupils or groups, and they can be used at any time and in any order. The task cards involve pupils in following instructions and completing a task independently.

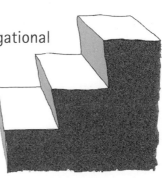

HOW TO USE THIS BOOK

QUICK STARTS

Quick starts are ideal warm-up activities for the beginning of a lesson, similar in principle to the starter activities at the beginning of the daily maths lesson. The activities are designed to be used flexibly: they can be used in any order and at any time, for example, during circle time. Each activity is intended to provide 10–15 minutes of group or whole class discussion.

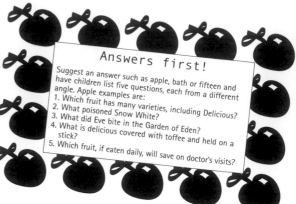

Answers first!

Suggest an answer such as apple, bath or fifteen and have children list five questions, each from a different angle. Apple examples are:
1. Which fruit has many varieties, including Delicious?
2. What poisoned Snow White?
3. What did Eve bite in the Garden of Eden?
4. What is delicious covered with toffee and held on a stick?
5. Which fruit, if eaten daily, will save on doctor's visits?

Example

Answers first! (page 11) could be used as a group activity. Divide the class into four, five or six groups and ask each group to write five questions for a particular answer word. The group can then read the questions one at a time to the rest of the class who try to guess the answer.

BLM 2   NAME Jack Davies

What is on the road?

Next to each letter of the alphabet write at least one thing that starts with that letter and that you might find beside or on the road. For example A – ant, ambulance, artwork, arch.

A	Ants	N	Nikol
B	Bus	O	old pepol
C	cat	P	pepel
D	dad car nal	Q	quiet pepol
E	egle	R	Rist Rani
F	grog	S	Sweat
G	gate	T	Trap
H	tumis	U	un lucky pepol

ACTIVITY BANK

These photocopiable activities can be used by individuals, groups or the whole class (with each child or pair of children referring to a copy of the sheet). An activity could provide the focus for a whole lesson (most of the activities require 30–40 minutes' investigation).

Example

What is on the road? (page 17) is an alphabetical activity with a difference that will improve children's vocabulary and fluency of ideas. You could repeat the activity for other places, for example, 'What is in the park?' or 'What is in the sports stadium?'

CHALLENGES

These activities are perfect for use in learning centres, in the school library or in the classroom. The investigational nature of the activities is in line with National Curriculum requirements such as AT1 in Maths and Science, and supports the development of investigational problem-solving skills.

Example

Design a pick-it-up tool (page 48) can provide the context for imaginative and challenging Design and Technology work. Discuss the range of applications that the tool could have for elderly or disabled people.

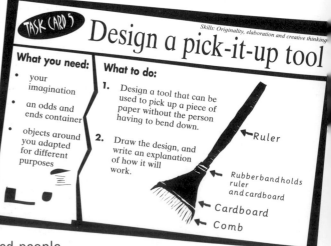

TASK CARD 5   Skills: Originality, elaboration and creative thinking

Design a pick-it-up tool

What you need:
- your imagination
- an odds and ends container
- objects around you adapted for different purposes

What to do:
1. Design a tool that can be used to pick up a piece of paper without the person having to bend down.
2. Draw the design, and write an explanation of how it will work.

Ruler

Rubber band holds ruler and cardboard

Cardboard

Comb

TEACHERS' FILE

What are thinking skills?

As well as helping children to think clearly, thinking skills enable them to collect information critically and creatively and to use this information to solve problems. Pupils also become more aware of decision-making processes as they develop their thinking skills. Through the activities in this book, children will learn thinking skills that encourage them to look at a variety of ideas, investigate in greater depth, practise more critical decision-making, challenge accepted ideas, approach tasks in decisive ways and search for misunderstandings, while keeping the aims of the task clearly in mind. As a result, their decisions will be more reliable, they will have a deeper understanding of concepts, their ideas will be more creative, they will examine content more critically and their work will be more carefully crafted.

Why do children need to develop thinking skills?

Children need to be able to judge, analyse and think critically in order to participate fully in a democratic and technological society. This can be achieved if the school as a whole recognises the value of thinking skills and provides opportunities for the thinking processes to be modelled and developed. All pupils can improve their thinking abilities, regardless of age, race, socio-economic status or different learning modes.

The basic skills are generally regarded as literacy and numeracy. These involve processes such as computation, recall of facts and the basic mechanics of writing. Once these fundamental skills have been mastered, children need to move on to more challenging tasks that will help them to understand more complex ideas. It is not necessarily true that pupils who can find the correct answers to problems have learnt thinking skills. Pupils need plenty of practice before they can tackle problems that require them to use advanced thinking skills. The cognitive operations that make up thinking need to be explored, explained, taught and practised many times before they can be mastered.

Some basic tips

Allow students to be nonconforming and encourage them to complete tasks in their own way. Encourage them to take risks, challenge ideas and to reflect on tasks. If a child learns hundreds of facts but hasn't developed the ability to explore possibilities, much of the knowledge they gain will be wasted.

Thinking 'domains'

Thinking skills can be divided into different areas, or thinking 'domains'. Children need experience of a variety of domains, because each domain has separate aims and develops particular skills. This book offers practice in the following key domains:

- **Critical thinking** encourages children to examine, clarify and evaluate an idea, belief or action. Pupils learn to infer, generalise, take a point of view, hypothesise and find temporary solutions.
- **Decision-making and problem-solving** involve processes such as brainstorming, linking ideas, using analogies, creating original ideas, organising information and looking at a problem from different perspectives. These techniques will enable children to find a variety of solutions to a problem.
- The ability to **collect, retain, recall and use information** when needed is another vital skill.
- **Creative thinking** encourages children to come up with original ideas.

Thinking processes

The activities in this book cover eight processes that are important in promoting thinking skills. These processes can be grouped into cognitive (thinking) and affective (feeling) abilities.

Cognitive abilities
- **Fluency** - thinking of as many ideas as possible
- **Flexibility** - looking at problems from different perspectives; thinking of ways to combine ideas into a new and different solution; grouping objects according to different criteria
- **Originality** - producing unusual or unique ideas
- **Elaboration** - adding or further developing ideas

Affective abilities
- **Curiosity** - working out an idea by instinctively following a certain route
- **Complexity** - thinking of more complex ways of approaching a task by searching for links, looking for missing sections or restructuring ideas
- **Risk-taking** - making guesses; defending ideas without fear of what others may think
- **Imagining** - picturing and describing something that has never occurred; imagining oneself in other times and places

ASSESSMENT

Allow time for the children to complete activities and give them opportunities to share their ideas in a group. One way in which pupils learn is by mirroring the behaviour and responses of others.
The following are general guidelines for assessing work:
- Display good pieces of work rather than grading them
- Avoid criticising pupils' responses or drawings
- Find something to value whenever possible.

Try to achieve continuity in the way pupils are assessed, so that information on each child is cumulative and accurate. A progressive file for each child can include details of their strengths, weaknesses and any special achievements. Note carefully any changes, progress or unusual results, especially in highly creative areas such as story-writing, art, special projects, research, inventions or music. Encourage pupils to examine and assess their own abilities and goals, to gain insight into themselves and the way they tackle problems. You could award fun certificates for proficiency in thinking skills (see page 44).

The classroom environment

The classroom environment can be arranged to allow children to express themselves creatively in tasks, exploration and play. It is helpful to organise materials systematically so that pupils have easy access to them. Use open shelving, plastic boxes and cartons for storing activities and resources. Flexible working and seating areas offer children freedom to move around to different areas of the classroom according to the tasks they are completing. If possible, provide separate areas for independent work, small group work and for the whole class to meet. Try changing the shape of these areas to create interest. You could encourage the children to solve problems using shapes such as hexagons, pentagons, spheres and domes in activities that involve making patterns or building towers.

Colours can be used to set the mood for the type of work pupils will be doing in a particular area of the classroom. Red stimulates thought and orange has an energising effect, while yellow should vitalise the children and speed up mental activity. Green and blue are soothing colours that may calm over-excited children. These colours are ideal to incorporate in a quiet reading area.

Thinking skills learning centres

A thinking skills learning centre could be set up in part of the classroom or as a shared resource for the whole school, perhaps in part of the school library. The learning centre might contain games, puzzles, relevant books and a computer with programs for developing thinking skills. It is a good idea to set up folders of blank worksheets and add new ones regularly. Building materials such as Lego® could be available for constructing unusual objects and devices. You could also provide a book in which pupils can record discoveries or useful tips for pupils working there in future.

Ways to enhance the learning environment

Improve the classroom layout and use displays as visual stimuli.

- Select teaching methods and organisational strategies appropriate to the pupils' needs
- Create a learning environment of high challenge and low stress
- Establish a positive, welcoming atmosphere
- Vary the way pupils work – for example, independently or in small groups
- Aim for a balance between structured and unstructured tasks
- Use a variety of learning styles – for example, hands on, visual, oral, written
- Establish the 'big picture' by linking tasks with pupils' experiences
- Use music to enhance the learning environment and to improve the children's ability to recall information

ICT TIPS

Pupils can be motivated by computer games that allow them to show commitment to a task. Simulation or strategy software encourages children to approach tasks open-mindedly and involves players in critical thinking, risk-taking and real life problem-solving.

ICT skills can be integrated into many aspects of learning. ICT is useful for developing problem-solving skills and the associated thinking skills through the use of existing educational software. Spreadsheets and databases can help children to learn more advanced skills, while developing lateral thinking and spatial orientation.

Computer versions of board games can also be used to develop thinking skills. Games such as chess and Scrabble® require children to learn rules and use a variety of strategies.

PARENT INVOLVEMENT

It is beneficial to inform parents that their children are learning thinking skills, as well as encouraging them to support their children's learning at home. Explain that thinking skills enable children to deal with complex situations using a range of thinking strategies, and will equip them to continue learning throughout their lives. On a practical level, parents' help can be enlisted in gathering unusual games and puzzles for a thinking skills learning centre (see page 8).

Parents can help their children to develop thinking skills in many ways, for example: providing opportunities to solve problems creatively; involving the children in planning family outings that take into consideration the needs of all family members; and allowing children to participate in family projects such as redesigning rooms. Most importantly, parents can encourage children to be individuals simply by listening to their ideas. Even if the ideas are unusual or impractical, parents can reassure children that their input is valuable. Children will benefit from being part of a family environment where it is acceptable to make mistakes, and where the emphasis is on learning from those mistakes.

QUICK STARTS

Answers first!

Suggest an answer such as apple, bath or 15 and have children list five questions, each from a different angle. Apple examples are:
1. Which fruit has many varieties, including Delicious?
2. What poisoned Snow White?
3. What did Eve bite in the Garden of Eden?
4. What is delicious covered with toffee and held on a stick?
5. Which fruit, if eaten daily, will save on doctor's visits?

What if?

Encourage pupils to explore alternatives by imagining they had the ability to change three things in their lives.
- What three things would they change?
- What would they change them to?
- How would this affect their lives?

Brainstorm!

Have groups of pupils brainstorm these topics:
- Imagine they are cold. What are possible reasons?
- Why might pupils be unable to play?
- Invent 20 reasons why school holidays might be doubled in length.

No answers are right or wrong and the aim is quantity not quality. Groups share their answers with the class so pupils can learn from different thinking.

Squiggles

Give pupils a square of paper to divide into four equal parts in as many ways as possible. Once students have explored horizontal and vertical lines, they can experiment making divisions using diagonals and curved lines. Then single line drawings can be developed into ideas. For example, an oval shape can have lines added to it to become a more interesting object. Rectangles, triangles, diamonds and trapeziums can be modified.

SCUMPS

S stands for **shape** of an object
C stands for **colour** of an object
U stands for **use** of an object
M stands for **material** an object is made from
P stands for **parts** of an object
S stands for **size** of an object

Ask pupils to use the SCUMPS process to list similarities and differences between a zebra and a boat.

Crazy combinations

Write somewhere pupils can see the five **S** words: **Smell** (odour), **Sound** (noise it makes), **Sense** (taste), **Size** (height, width, weight, depth), **Speciality** (use).

Pair pupils and ask them to use the five **S** words to list the attributes of a flower, a dog and a bicycle. Then ask them to combine some of these attributes into a new object. Have them draw, describe and name the new object.

My theme park

Have children design and name their own theme park. Pupils should write the rules and regulations they feel are important for the running of the park, and explain why these are necessary. What rides would they have? How would their theme park be different from parks that already exist? What improvements could they make to the present parks?

How do you do it?

Ask pupils to list as many ways as they can think of to:
- Turn the bedroom light on and off from their bed
- Wash the dog
- Remove rubbish from the playground

Eggs galore

- Have the children close their eyes and imagine that they are inside an egg. Ask them to think about and describe how they feel.
- Ask pupils to design an eggshell peeler. Have them draw their invention and explain it to the class.
- What use could the eggshell be put to?

Inventing a robot

Ask pupils to design a robot that will be able to meet their needs in the future. Explain that robots do not have to resemble people, so students can be very creative. Pupils should write a user's manual for their robot, explaining the function that each feature of the robot will perform. Display the designs and discuss with the class.

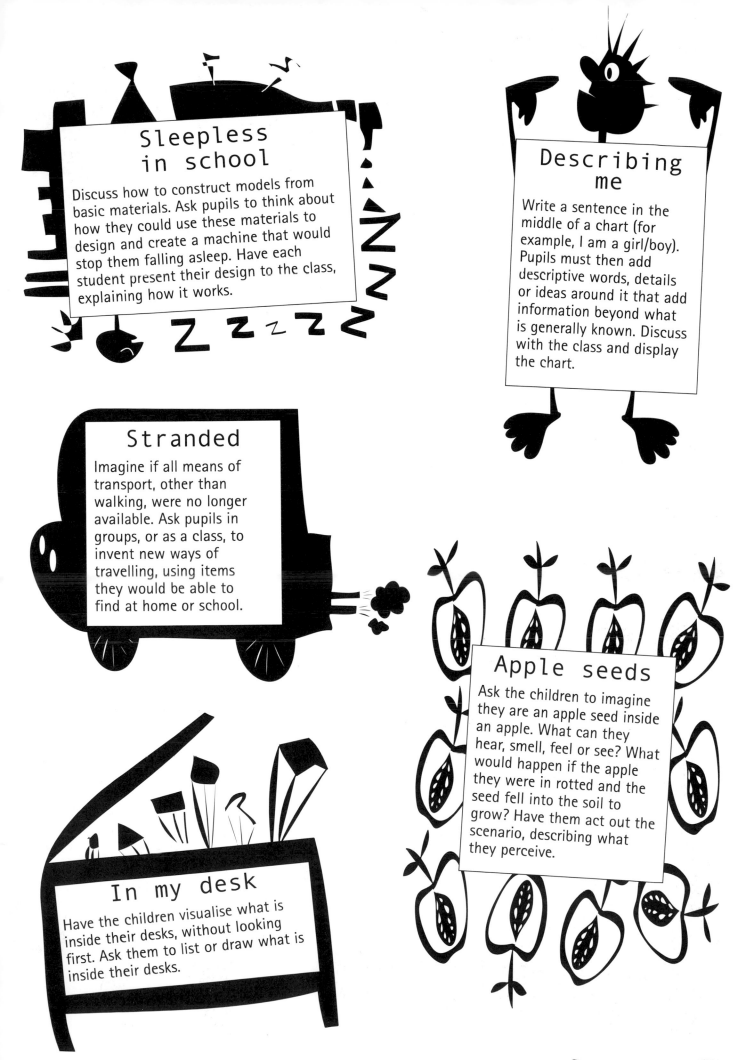

Sleepless in school

Discuss how to construct models from basic materials. Ask pupils to think about how they could use these materials to design and create a machine that would stop them falling asleep. Have each student present their design to the class, explaining how it works.

Describing me

Write a sentence in the middle of a chart (for example, I am a girl/boy). Pupils must then add descriptive words, details or ideas around it that add information beyond what is generally known. Discuss with the class and display the chart.

Stranded

Imagine if all means of transport, other than walking, were no longer available. Ask pupils in groups, or as a class, to invent new ways of travelling, using items they would be able to find at home or school.

Apple seeds

Ask the children to imagine they are an apple seed inside an apple. What can they hear, smell, feel or see? What would happen if the apple they were in rotted and the seed fell into the soil to grow? Have them act out the scenario, describing what they perceive.

In my desk

Have the children visualise what is inside their desks, without looking first. Ask them to list or draw what is inside their desks.

Green!

Ask pupils to draw what they could be if they were green. Possible answers are grass, a frog, aliens, jelly, a traffic light. Have pupils work in groups to combine some of the attributes of these objects to make a new green object, which they should name.

BAR

B makes an object bigger or smaller

A adds something on to an object

R replaces, changes or rearranges an object

BAR is useful for reinventing everyday objects. Ask the children to use the BAR process to redesign a boat or a house, or improve a spoon. They can then improve a pencil case so that it becomes more appealing to children.

SCAMPER

S Can anything be substituted?
C Can ideas, events or contents be combined?
A Can anything be adapted?
M Can anything be modified, magnified or minimised?
P Can the purpose be changed?
E Can anything be eliminated?
R Reverse the pace, order of events and manner.

SCAMPER encourages pupils to look at alternatives. Ask them to apply this strategy to a rubber, ruler, water bottle, orange, toy or game.

Supermarket categories

Ask pupils to make a list of words about food. Photocopy their lists and cut them up. Pupils, in groups, are given a set of these words. Words should be grouped into categories and then regrouped into alternative categories. Take pupils on an excursion to a supermarket and discuss different ways in which the manager has categorised products. Ask if students can suggest practical alternatives.

Look alike

Choose three pupils who have something in common. This could be a haircut, item of clothing, trainers or a watch. Ask other pupils to classify the group according to some characteristics.

Is that red?

Speech bubble: Yummy! Red nectarines are delicious.

List or draw all the red objects that you can think of. Try to think about the colour from a different point of view or as a result of an action, for example, when someone blushes. See who can make the longest list.

Thinking skill: Fluency

What is on the road?

Next to each letter of the alphabet write at least one thing that starts with that letter and that you might find beside or on the road. For example, A – ant, ambulance, artwork, arch.

A _____ N _____

B _____ O _____

C _____ P _____

D _____ Q _____

E _____ R _____

F _____ S _____

G _____ T _____

H _____ U _____

I _____ V _____

J _____ W _____

K _____ X _____

L _____ Y _____

M _____ Z _____

Thinking skill: Fluency

Catch the elephant

Work in a group of three or four. List ways you can think of to catch an elephant that has escaped from the zoo. Try to think of creative and unusual ways by adding to the ideas of others in your group.

Thinking skill: Fluency

Make them interesting!

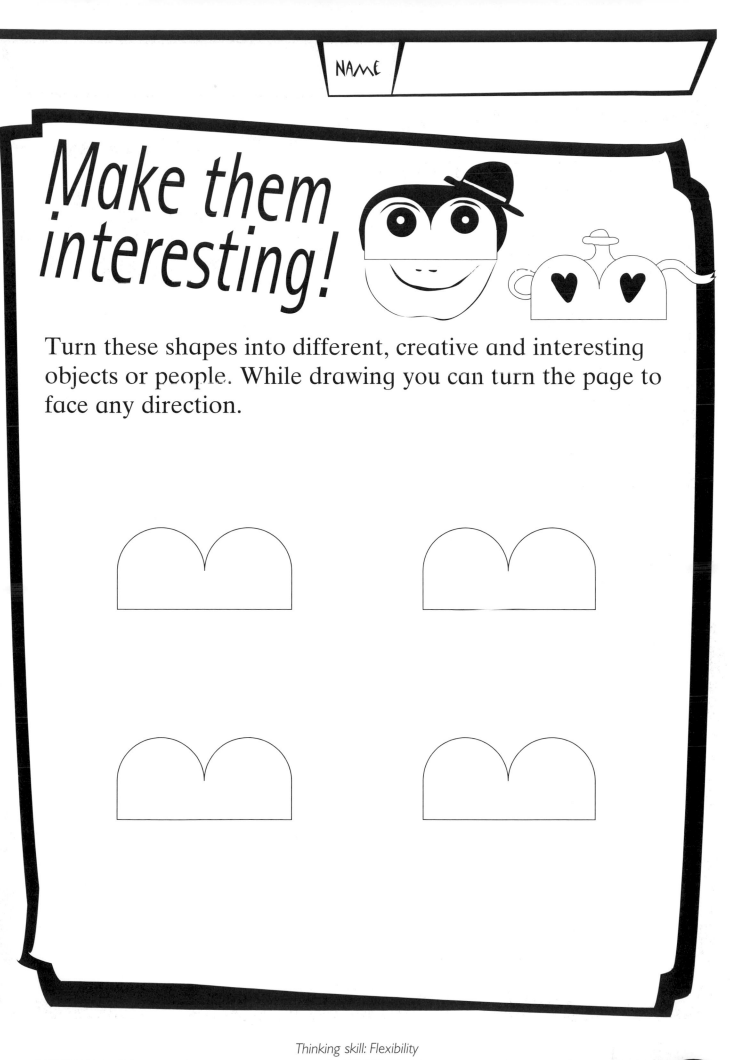

Turn these shapes into different, creative and interesting objects or people. While drawing you can turn the page to face any direction.

Thinking skill: Flexibility

Street safety

Think of different ways to make cars and other traffic travel more slowly and more cautiously on your street. Explain and draw your suggestions.

Thinking skill: Flexibility

Listing ideas

Working in a group of two or three, brainstorm these ideas. See which group can develop the most ideas for each list.

List objects that have a handle.

_____

_____

_____

_____

List words to do with feeling happy.

_____

_____

_____

List three-syllable words (*for example, ex-cite-ment*).

_____

_____

_____

_____

_____

List as many rhyming couplets as you can (*for example, a black sack, a big pig*).

_____

_____

_____

_____

_____

Thinking skill: Flexibility

NAME

How can you use it?

List possible uses for a milk carton.

_____

_____

_____

_____

_____

_____

_____

_____

_____

_____

_____

How can a piece of string be used for each of these activities or functions?

To play a sport?	To play a game?	As an item of clothing?

Thinking skill: Flexibility

What can it be?

Insert the name of at least one food for each question.

This food is shaped like a football. _____

This food is two colours, one
outside and the other inside. _____

This food comes in a bag. _____

You cannot eat this food with a fork. _____

This food makes a noise when it is cooked. _____

List three things that you can never touch.

_____

_____

_____

List three things that you can never wash.

_____

_____

_____

List three things that you could never see at a zoo.

_____

_____

_____

Thinking skill: Flexibility

NAME

Change these shapes

Create interesting objects from these shapes. Below
each drawing explain what you have drawn.

Thinking skill: Imaginative visualisation

Moving around

Work in a group of four. Your group should choose a means of transport, for example, a Tyrannosaurus Rex, ambulance, helicopter, donkey, sled, pram, bicycle, car, camel, or horse and carriage. Your task is to improve that way of travelling. Draw or describe each change you make and give explanations for the changes.

Your means of transport:	
Changes	Reasons

Thinking skill: Imaginative visualisation

What is this?

Can you find the connection or link between the two objects on each line?

If ☀ is the sun, what could this be ♡ ? _____

If ⊤ is a street sign, what is this ⟳ ? _____

If ◯ is a yoyo, what is | ? _____

If ● is a piece of popcorn, what is ⏝ ? _____

If ◯ is a noise, what could ⌒ be? _____

List all the uses for toothpicks.

_____
_____
_____

_____
_____
_____
_____

List uses for a metal coat hanger. Choose one object on the list and make it.

_____
_____
_____
_____
_____

Thinking skill: Originality and elaboration

What a ladder!

1. Dog kennel.

2. Make it **B**igger. This will give the dog more room.

3. **A**dd bedding and windows for greater comfort.

4. **R**eplace the simple wooden walls with brick for better insulation against the cold.

Redesign the stepladder using BAR. Draw and explain each change.

B Make it bigger

Reasons: ....

....

A Add something

Reasons: ....

....

R Replace, change or rearrange

Reasons: ....

....

Thinking skill: Originality and elaboration

What a racket!

1. Glasses

2. Make lenses **B**igger so frames don't interfere with vision.

3. **A**dd small sunshades, so sun doesn't get in eyes.

4. **R**eplace earpieces with elastic, so glasses stay on when playing a sport.

Design a new and improved tennis racket using BAR to help you. Draw and explain each change.

B Make it bigger

Reasons: ....
....

A Add something

Reasons: ....
....

R Replace, change or rearrange

Reasons: ....
....

Thinking skill: Originality and elaboration

A new body

If you had the task of redesigning the human body, think about the changes you could make. Draw the 'changed body' and list the advantages of the new design. You can use BAR, SCAMPER or another creative approach for the task.

Design

Advantages

Thinking skill: Originality and elaboration

Create a new cage

Help redesign this monkey's cage.
You can use BAR, SCAMPER or
another creative approach for the
task. Draw and explain each change.

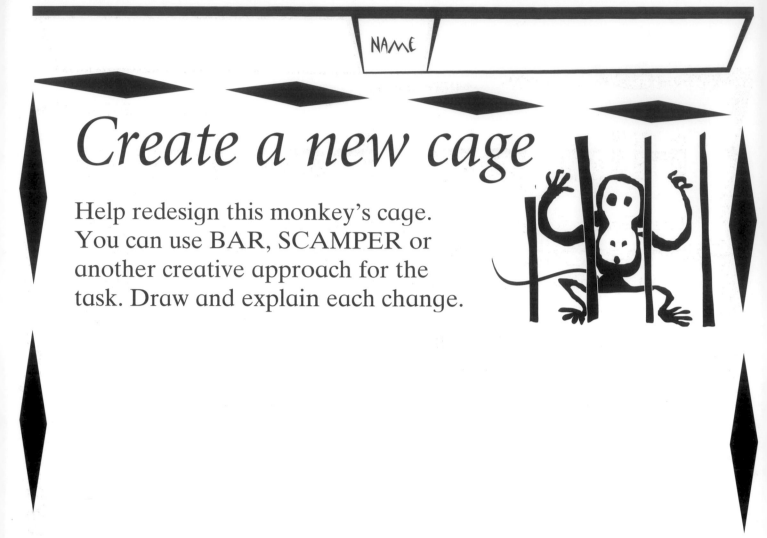

Thinking skill: Originality and elaboration

Hip pip hooray!

The Green family farms mangoes. This year
they had a bumper crop. The flesh of the fruit
is cut off and canned in a nearby factory.
Unfortunately, they have all the stones from
the mangoes left over and the Greens don't
know what to do with them. List or draw
suggestions for how they could use the stones.

Thinking skill: Originality and elaboration

Clean up!

Create a 'clean up the garden' machine. Draw it and explain how it works.

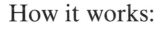

How it works:

_____

_____

_____

_____

_____

_____

_____

_____

Thinking skill: Creative thinking

Redesign an object

Work with a partner. Choose an object (or a
picture of an object) that you could redesign.
It could be a spade, a kitchen utensil such as
tongs, a colander, a whisk, a spoon or a fork.

Describe what the object is used for.

_____

_____

_____

_____

Brainstorm other uses.

_____

_____

_____

_____

Imagine that the object was remade a hundred times larger. What uses
would it have now?

_____

_____

_____

Choose one part of the object to change. List its new uses.

_____

_____

_____

Reverse or rearrange part of the object. On the back of this sheet, draw
what it looks like now.

Thinking skill: Creative thinking

Find a connection

Here's the problem: The holiday camp has been poorly attended. Use a word processor, a packet of crisps, a T-shirt and a dog to create a way to get more people to go.

_____

_____

_____

_____

_____

_____

_____

_____

_____

Reflection: Which of the ideas should be acted on? What should be done?

_____

_____

Thinking skill: Creative thinking

My new invention!

Use this shape as the basis for a new invention.

Draw the invention. Write its name on the line below your drawing.

What is it used for?

Thinking skill: Creative thinking

A time capsule

Imagine that you have to choose 10 personal items to fit in a time capsule. You have been asked to choose items that would use each of the senses. What would you include? Explain the reasons for each choice.

Choice	Reasons

You are allowed to write a 30-word message to go in your time capsule. What would you like people to know about this time and the way you live? Draft the message on scrap paper and write the finished text on the back of this sheet.

Thinking skill: Creative thinking

NAME

Redesign your classroom

Improve your classroom so that it becomes a more unusual and exciting place to be. Begin by listing what you do not like about the room and then think creatively about the changes that you can make.

Things I do not like

_____

_____

_____

_____

_____

Changes I would make

_____

_____

_____

_____

_____

_____

Thinking skill: Creative thinking

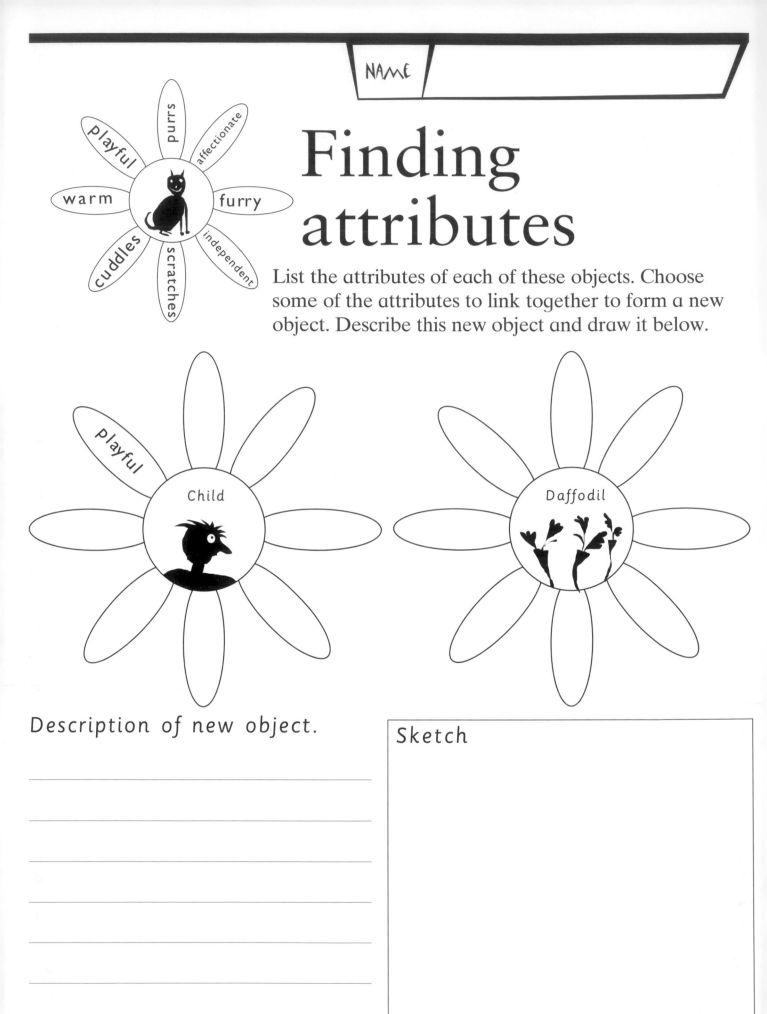

Finding attributes

List the attributes of each of these objects. Choose some of the attributes to link together to form a new object. Describe this new object and draw it below.

Child

Daffodil

Description of new object.

Sketch

Thinking skill: Creative thinking

Create something new

List the attributes of traffic lights and telephones. Combine some of them into a new object. Use the five S word strategy to help you.

Traffic lights	Telephones
Smell:_____	Smell:_____
Sound:_____	Sound:_____
Sense: _____	Sense: _____
Size: _____	Size: _____
Speciality:_____	Speciality:_____

New object

Thinking skill: Creative thinking

What a question!

This is a happy line leaping and bounding along!

Draw a silly line.

Draw a sad line.

The answer is 'no'. Write three questions.

_____

_____

_____

List reasons why the people were laughing and shouting.

_____

_____

_____

You cannot see out of the windows. List the possible reasons.

_____

_____

_____

Why can't you open the door? Think of possible reasons.

_____

_____

_____

Thinking skill: Questioning

Finding categories

Divide these objects into groups (at least two items per group). Label each group with a description (for example 'articles of clothing'). The five S word strategy can help when forming groups. The five S words are Smell, Sound, Sense, Size and Speciality.

rice   eggs   coin   scratch   wink   doughnut
toaster   beans   soldier   smile   cheese   eyebrows
scissors   legs   nail   sun   rub   ears   envelope
pilot   frown   itch   box   tin   nurse   rose
stamp   hat   folder   teacher

Groups:

Thinking skill: Categorising

Sort them

Work in a group of three. Each member of the group must look for and collect five objects from an area specified by your teacher. Put all 15 collected objects on a table. In your group, take turns to sort the objects into sets. Describe your sets below. Then talk about them with the rest of your group. Count how many sets you have altogether. Make sure similar sets are only counted once. (You could use the five S word or SCUMPS strategies to help sort the items into sets.)

List and describe your sets.

_____

_____

_____

_____

_____

Add the sets that others found.

_____

_____

_____

_____

_____ **Total number**

_____ **of sets**

_____

_____

_____

Thinking skill: Categorising

Character sketch

Think of all the adjectives that could be used to describe a character you know or have read about in a book. List these adjectives below. Think about how you can classify and group them. Remember there must be at least two words per group.

Adjective lists

Group classification

Thinking skill: Categorising

Thinking skills awards

Awarded to _____

Wow! That's original!

Signed _____

Date _____

Awarded to _____

Quite a question!

Signed _____

Date _____

Awarded to _____

Tops in thinking skills!

Signed _____

Date _____

Creative thinker!

Awarded to _____

Signed _____

Date _____

CHALLENGES

TASK CARD 1

View the zoo

What you need:

- 1 metre string
- 1 metre masking tape
- 30 straws
- a few sheets of newspaper

What to do:

1. Build a bridge that can be used to look down on the animals in a zoo.

2. What is the strongest shape for the bridge?

3. How will you create the supports? How will it balance?

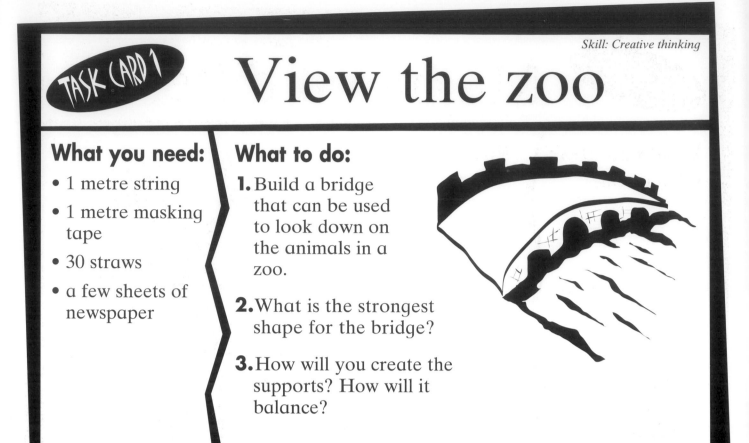

TASK CARD 2

Play the game

What you need:

- a piece of cardboard
- pencil
- scrap paper
- a die
- coloured counters
- an atlas (optional)

What to do:

1. Develop a board game using a map, at least five places to visit, one die and a number of counters. Use a different setting for each place that you visit – a volcano, a desert, a sea, a river, a mountain, a village, a city, outer space. How can you jump and move ahead? Will you have bonus cards? What traps can you fall into that will force you to move backwards? How will you number the board? How many people can play at a time?

2. Draw your plan on scrap paper before you begin.

3. Now do a good copy of your game on cardboard and decorate it.

4. Write rules that are clear and simple, and play the game with some friends.

Making it different

What you need:

- 3 magazines to cut up
- one sheet of A3 paper
- glue
- a pair of scissors

What to do:

1. Work in small groups. As a group, choose six pictures of objects to cut out.

2. Cut, trim and glue the six pictures together to make a new object.

3. Name the object.

4. List the features of the new object, thinking of as many as possible.

Code it

What you need:

- paper
- ink
- inkpad
- pencil
- spy hat (optional)

What to do:

1. Make up a spy code and write a secret message. Exchange your message with others.

2. Write a spy cartoon using your code. Make the characters out of fingerprints. Fill at least eight cartoon squares.

The goose flies backwards at midnight.

Thgindim ta sdrawkcab seilf esoog eht.

Hi!

Password?

TASK CARD 5 — Design a pick-it-up tool

What you need:

- your imagination
- an odds and ends container
- objects around you adapted for different purposes

What to do:

1. Design a tool that can be used to pick up a piece of paper without the person having to bend down.

2. Draw the design and write an explanation of how it will work.

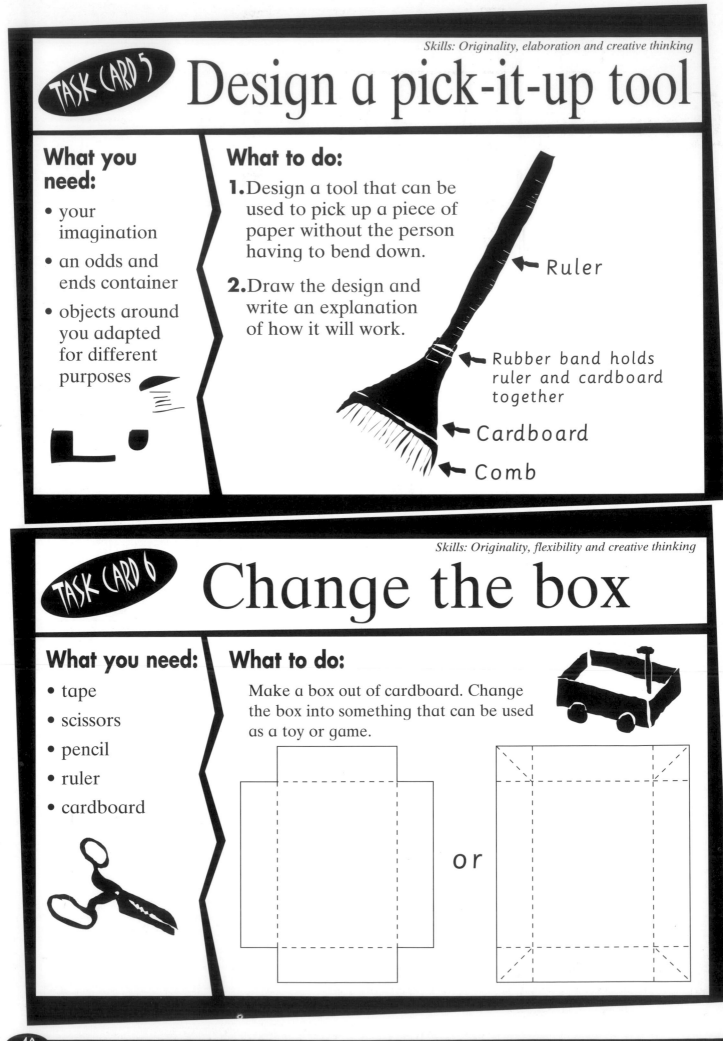

Ruler

Rubber band holds ruler and cardboard together

Cardboard

Comb

TASK CARD 6 — Change the box

What you need:

- tape
- scissors
- pencil
- ruler
- cardboard

What to do:

Make a box out of cardboard. Change the box into something that can be used as a toy or game.

or